This book is dedicated to Aline and William
"Bras de Fer"

**The author of this book Benjamin James
Baillie lives and works in Normandy**

THE SEA WOLVES

The Viking creation of Normandy and its iron Dukes

911 – 1087 AD

By Benjamin James Baillie

Contents

Rollo (Hrolfr) Founder of
Normandy 911 A.D

Introduction

For over two centuries the Norman conquests created a piecemeal Empire that stretched from the wild windswept landscapes of Celtic Ireland and Scotland in the north to the sun drenched shores of Sicily in the Mediterranean and to the very frontiers of Christendom itself in the Outremer (Holy land). However the story of the Normans started in the early 10th century in Northern France, where Viking raiders from Scandinavia settled down and created Normandy land of the North men , which became one of the most feared and organised Principalities in medieval Europe.

The sea wolves

For three centuries Europe was terrorised by a fierce warrior race from Scandinavia that became known to us as the Vikings. The origin of the word Viking itself is far from clear, but it represented the

Viking ship stone carving, Sweden

Northern peoples from Norway, Sweden, and Denmark who ventured out in their dragon head ships to raid and trade during the last three centuries of the first millennium.

Due to over population and other factors in their traditional homelands, the Viking age of expansion commenced just before the beginning of the ninth century.

The Norwegians and the Danes naturally sailed west and south towards the British Isles and Western Europe. The Swedes crossed the Baltic Sea and infiltrated into Poland, the Baltic States and Russia creating the Viking Kingdom of Rus (Novagrad). Using their famous longboats which could hold up to 50 warriors, the Vikings were able to navigate the open seas with ease and sail up the sallowest rivers wherever they went.

They travelled far and wide from North Africa and the Mediterranean to the inland rivers of the Dniepner and Volga in central Russia where they became known as Varangians. They even formed the Varangian guard (bodyguards of the Byzantine Emperor in Constantinople). Perhaps their greatest expedition was setting foot on North American soil, some 500 years before Christopher Columbus.

The Oseberg Viking ship, Norway

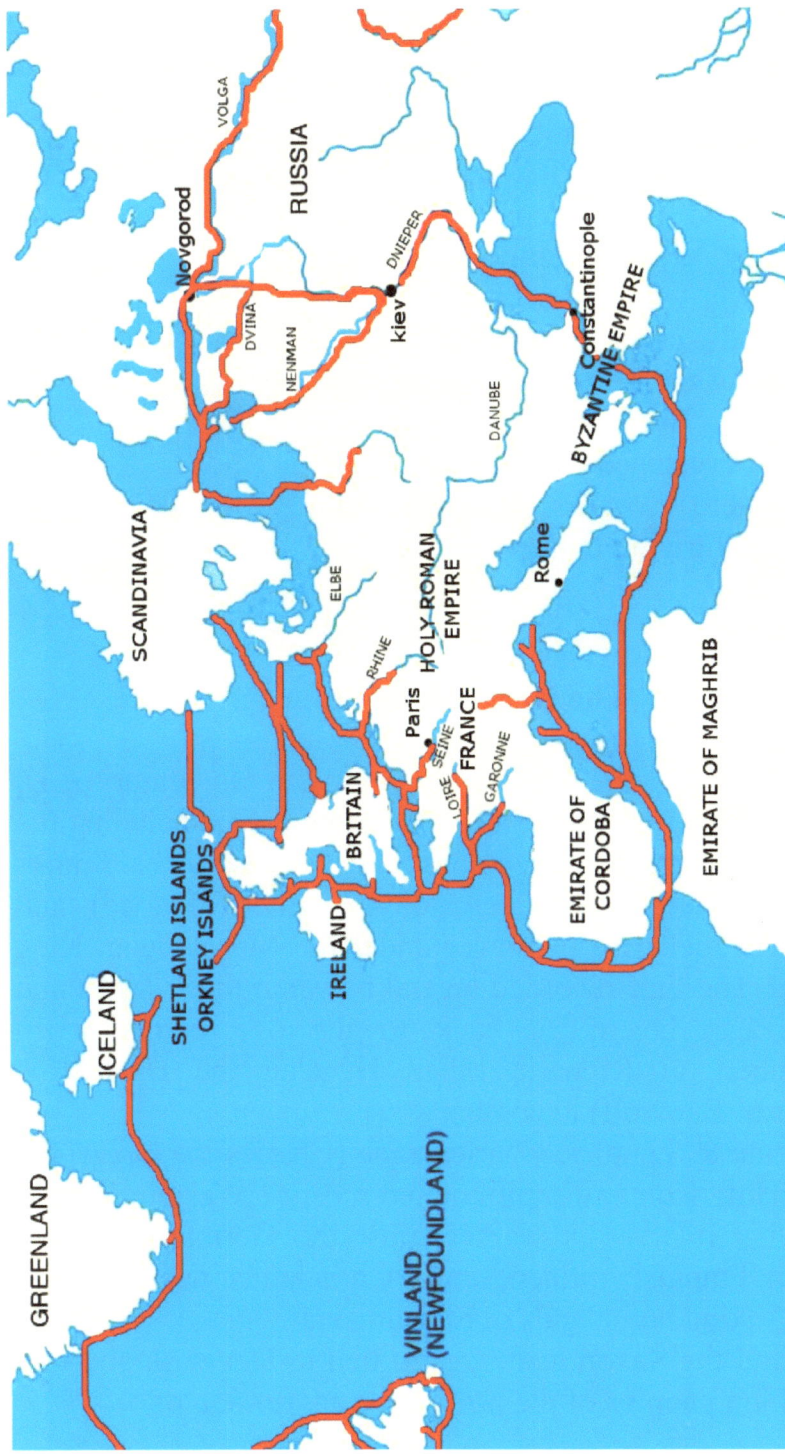

VIKING EXPLORATION MAP 750-1066 A.D

GREENLAND

ICELAND

SHETLAND ISLANDS
ORKNEY ISLANDS

IRELAND

BRITAIN

VINLAND
(NEWFOUNDLAND)

SCANDINAVIA

Novgorod

VOLGA

RUSSIA

DVINA

NENMAN

DNIEPER

kiev

DANUBE

ELBE

HOLY ROMAN
EMPIRE

RHINE

Paris

SEINE

FRANCE

LOIRE

GARONNE

Rome

BYZANTINE EMPIRE

Constantinople

EMIRATE OF
CORDOBA

EMIRATE OF MAGHRIB

VIKING ROUTES

The Viking Conquests, France

The Viking expeditions had three main goals, trading, raiding and later conquest. When the crews returned to Scandinavia with their spoils of booty and slaves they spread the word of the riches that were on offer. By the late 9th century, organised bands and armies were crossing the seas intent on outright conquest.

11th century Viking warrior head carving

The Kingdom of France

After the fall of the Roman Empire in the 5th century A.D, Gaul was overrun by various Germanic tribes including the Visigoths, Burgundians, Alans and Franks. The Franks occupied Neustria (modern day Northern France) and continued their rise to power under the Merovingian King Clovis. The first recorded legend between the Vikings and Franks can be traced back to the 6th century when Theudebert of Ripuaria killed Hygelac the Dane (the brother of Beowolf) in combat.

In the late 8th century, Charlemagne (Charles the Great) the future Holy Roman Empire united most of Western Europe under his rule. His wars against the Germanic Saxons brought Frankish influence and Christianity nearer to the pagan Viking homelands of Scandinavia.

Widukind the Saxon leader, even fled to Denmark and told the Viking peoples of the power and aggression of

Charlemagne. The Vikings did not wait for a Frankish invasion and instead brought terror to the very heart of the Carolingian Empire.

France 799 A.D

In the year 799 A.D the Vikings attacked France for the first time near Noirmoutier (Vendée Region of Western France). They pillaged the monastery, striping it of its riches and killed the fleeing monks. Charlemagne ordered the construction of a fleet and defences to be erected on France s Western coastline. These measures kept the Norsemen at bay and France weathered the Viking raids until the death of Louis the Pious in 840 A.D

With the Frankish Empire in disarray, the Vikings took their chance and attacked France. The great inland rivers of the Seine, Loire, Garonne, Saone and the Rhine allowed the Vikings to infiltrate deep into the heart of the Kingdom. In 841 A.D they appeared in the Seine valley and pillaged the rich abbeys of Jumiéges and St Georges de Boucherville. The region s capital Rouen was also sacked and burned to the ground by the sea wolves.

The Seine valley from the Brotonne forest (Normandy, France)

Overleaf; depiction of a Viking raid in the Seine estuary

Ragnar s raid on Paris 845 A.D

The raids increased with ferocity during the 840s. In 845 A.D a Viking fleet of 120 longboats sailed the 240 miles from the sea to the French capital Paris. They were commanded by one of the most famous Vikings of them all; Ragnar Lodbrok hairy breaches . Ragnar s fame was legendary, and his exploits earned him a place as one of the most popular heroes in the Viking Sagas. After ravaging the city of Rouen his pagan war band continued upstream and sacked the modern day town of Chaussy near Paris.

The new Frankish King, Charles II the bald raised an army and set out to confront Ragnar s Vikings. He split his army on both sides of the Seine River hoping to encircle the Norsemen, but Ragnar realised what Charles was up to and quickly ambushed the smaller Frankish force, taking numerous prisoners and slaughtering the rest.

The Viking and their longboats from the "The Miracles of St Edmund" manuscript

The 111 unfortunate captured prisoners were taken and then executed on a tiny island in the middle of the Seine, in front of Charles and his remaining men who watched on helplessly. Ceasing the initiative again, Ragnar launched a second bold attack against the remainder of the Frankish forces. Charles fearing for his life fled the field with the remnants of his army and headed for the safety of St Denis.

With the Frankish forces destroyed, Rangnar terrorised the region, sacking towns, villages and wasting the land. On Easter Sunday 845 A.D the Vikings broke through the defences of the island city of Paris and plundered the capital. Charles who was still in St Denis behind the Vikings could have blocked off the Seine River and any escape route open to them. Instead he hesitated, and paid Ragnar off with 7000 pounds of silver. Charles payment became known as the Dane geld (Danes pay) or simply, protection money to stop any further aggression. The marauding Scandinavians returned back down the river Seine to Denmark unmolested.

As for the Viking warlord Ragnar, legend has it that he met his end when he was shipwrecked on the English coast. After being captured by the Northumbrian King Ælla, he was thrown into a pit of Snakes and bitten to death.

Blood eagle execution from a Viking stone carving

His sons Halfdan, Björn Ironside, Sigurd Snake-in-the-Eye and Ivar the Boneless swore to avenge their father s death. In 865 A.D they invaded England with the Great Heathen Army and captured York. King Ælla was captured in battle outside the city walls and sentenced to death according to the tradition of the blood eagle (A cruel Viking method of torture and execution).

The great invasions 856-911

Although Charles had paid off one group of Vikings, within 7 years several roaming fleets and armies were attacking his Kingdom. Sometimes these war bands joined forces with each other, as was the case in 856 A.D when the Scandinavians ransacked Paris again. They were not adverse to accepting bribery or even being recruited by the feudal lords of medieval France in their private wars against the King and the other nobility.

King Charles II "the bald"

Just as in England, the Vikings were changing their behaviour and tactics. Raiding was slowly becoming invasion and colonisation. They were spending the winters on the coastal regions and estuaries of France. The island of Oselles (probably modern day Oissel) was fortified by the Vikings and used as a base to strike terror into the Parisian region. Also somewhere between Saint Wandrille and Jumiéges in the forest of Arélaune (now Brotonne) the raiders had a shipyard where they had access to a huge supply of wood and trees to repair and build their ships.

In the campaigning season they actively targeted the rich, but poorly defended centres of commerce. Every year they grew bolder in their ferocious military campaigns against the Carolingian Empire, forcing the Church and nobility to pay the Dane geld . Charles II position was so threatened that he sought to ally himself with the Anglo-Saxons of Wessex (England) in combating the Viking menace by marrying off his daughter Judith to Æthelwulf (King of Wessex).

Charles II had his successes during the 860s. His newly constructed fortifications on the river Seine and Marne succeeded in trapping Weland s Viking raiding party in 862 A.D. However, just four years later, the Franks were heavily defeated at Melun. When Charles died in 876 A.D the Viking attacks intensified, the united Empire of Charlemagne had disintegrated into fragmented Kingdoms, much easier for the Vikings to infiltrate.

The siege of Paris 885-886

In 885 A.D a massive Viking fleet, some say as large as 700 ships, sailed up the river Seine under the command of Siegfried. Their target was Paris, and the memories of Ragnar s devastating raid of 845 A.D was still fresh in the minds of the populace. Siegfried demanded the usual Dane geld bribe, but this time King Charles the Fat refused to pay it. The Frankish nobility including Odo (the Count of Paris) and Joscelin (the Abbot of St Germain des Prés) were tasked with defending the city against the pagan hordes.

Viking Warrior carving 9th century

In November, Siegfried s Vikings attacked the city walls with scaling ladders and battering rams. The battle was fierce, but the Franks repulsed the Norsemen with everything they had within their arsenal. Hot burning oil was poured down onto the attackers along with flaming arrows and stones hurled from the defensive battlements. Throughout the cold damp winter the Vikings besieged Paris and tried to enter the city by any means possible. In one such attempt they filled the city s moat with the bodies of the executed prisoners and used them as a sort of pontoon bridge to gain closer access to the Parisian fortified towers. In the New Year Count Odo managed to break through the Viking lines and get word to Charles (who was in Italy) of the situation and also requesting urgent assistance. The siege dragged on into the summer of 886 A.D with both sides refusing to give in.

By the time Charles arrived on the scene, both the defenders and attackers had been decimated by disease. Instead of attacking the remaining Vikings, one of whom may have been a certain Rollo the Ganger ; Charles offered them the Dane geld in return for recruiting them as mercenaries to crush a rebellion within the Empire.

Statue of Rollo, Rouen, Normandy

Gongu-Hrolfr / Rollo the Ganger(walker)

The question of the origin of Hrolf/Rollo is still disputed between Norway and Denmark to this day. Norwegian and Icelandic historians firmly believe that the identity of the famous Viking Jarl is Ganger Hrolf (Rollo the Walker). He earned his nickname the walker because no one could find a horse big enough to carry the giant Viking warlord, hence he walked everywhere. He is believed to have been a son of Rognvald Eysteinsson (the Norse Earl of More, Norway). After a dispute with the Norwegian King Harald Fairhair, Rollo was forced to leave his homeland and seek fame and fortune abroad.

Like many other Vikings, Rollo found his way to Northern France after raiding and pillaging in the Great Heathen army campaign of terror in Anglo-Saxon England. Slowly but surely he gained experience and became one of the main warlords of the late 9th century. Whether or not he was at the siege of Paris cannot be verified, but it is quite possible. What is certain is that by 911 A.D Rollo was in command of the Viking army that attacked Chartres.

The Siege of Chartres 911 A.D

In the spring of 911 A.D Rollo laid siege to the Frankish city of Chartres. The several thousand strong Viking army devastated the surrounding region before encircling the city. Their main camp was located just up steam on the island of Petits-Pres on the river Eure. Bishop Guateaume organised the defence of the city and sent out urgent calls for help to the Frankish King Charles III the simple and the local nobility. The strong walls and gallant resistance of the defenders thwarted the Viking assaults to take the city by storm. In July a Frankish army arrived on the scene to break the siege. According to the annals of Ste Colombe de Sens the two armies clashed in an epic confrontation just outside the city. After an initial Frankish charge, Viking berserkers forced the Franks back in the vicious hand to hand combat. A local legend says that the Vikings were forced to retreat when Bishop Guateaume and the garrison charged out of the city carrying Mary s Veil (a holy relic). Rollo ordered a fighting withdrawal towards a small hill known as Léves on the banks of the river Eure. With the arrival of Frankish reserves under the Count of Poitiers, the Franks began to close in on Rollo s men. As nightfall fell they encamped at the foot of the hill and prepared for a final showdown with the Viking invaders.

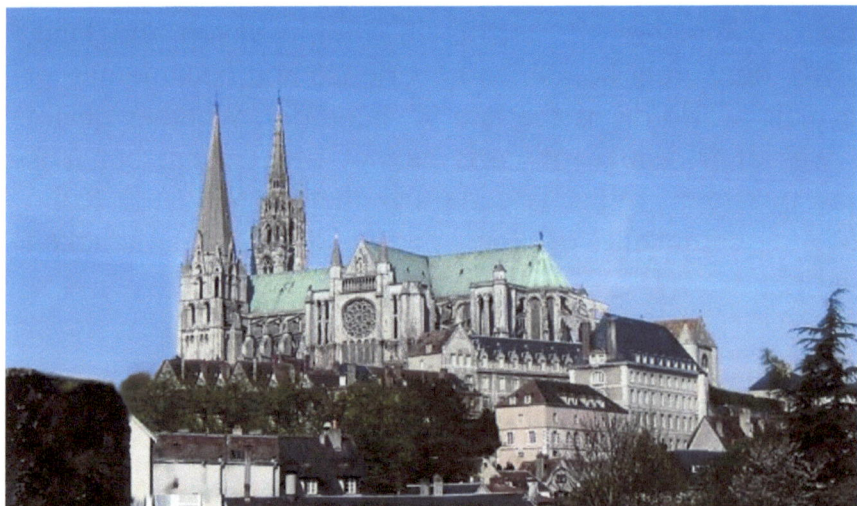

Chartres Cathedral, the medieval heart of the city

Rollo was faced utter annihilation unless he could change the fortunes of his army; the cunning warlord devised a plan to alter the dire situation. He ordered several hand picked warriors to conduct a stealth operation against his foes. The selected Vikings crept down the hill and infiltrated the Frankish camp. At the crucial moment they blew on their horns and tricked the Franks into believing that they were being attacked by the whole Viking army. The camp fell into complete panic, with horses and soldiers fleeing in all directions. Rollo s ruse had worked, while the Franks were in disarray he was able to slip away into the night with the remainder of the army to the safety of his ships.

In the morning the Frankish army marched out after the Vikings to give battle, but when they arrived towards the Norse position on the river Eure they were halted by a formidable barricade, hastily constructed out of dead animals, trees and bushes. The Franks may have relieved the siege of Chartres, but they had failed to eliminate Rollo s army. The Vikings were able to return back to the relative safety of Rouen and the Seine valley.

King Charles III decided to try and capitalise on the French victory at Chartres. He did not launch a military campaign against the Vikings, but instead sent emissaries on a diplomatic mission to Rollo s camp.

The Treaty of Saint Clair Sur Epte and the Creation of Normandy

According to Dudo de Saint Quentin (the 10th / 11th century historiographer to the Dukes of Normandy) Rollo and King Charles III met in the small town of Saint Clair sur Epte on the frontier of the Viking colony in 911A.D. King Charles III, accepting that he could not recover Rouen and the coastal regions of Neustria from the invaders, agreed to cede the land from the river Epte to the sea to Rollo if he became a vassal of the Frankish King and convert to Christianity. The terms were that Rollo would be given the title Count of Rouen and legitimately govern the land in the King s name. Charles hoped that by ceding the Pagi of Caux, Talon, Roumois, Evrecin and Vexin to Rollo, he would be creating a buffer state to protect France from further Viking attacks. Rollo agreed to the terms, but when he was asked to perform the act of homage and fealty he refused. Legend has it that to consecrate the Treaty he would have to kiss the King s foot. He replied that;

I will never kneel before another man, nor kiss anyone s foot

Rollo ordered one of his men to take his place and kiss the King s foot. The warrior knelt down and took the King s foot in his hands. Instead of kissing it, he hurled the King into the air; Charles III was thrown off his feet and fell over backwards. The scene caused an uproar of laughter amongst the Vikings. The land of the North-men Normandy had officially been created.

Depiction of the Treaty of Saint Clair Sur Epte

The creation of Normandy

Normandy and the iron Dukes 911-1087 A.D

For Charles the agreement proved to be success. There were no more Viking raids on his lands and Rollo kept his word and was baptised a Christian in 912 A.D, taking the name Robert. The Roujarl (Count of Rouen), as Rollo was known to his Viking followers, started to transform his new territory. Instead of sacking the churches and abbeys, he began to repair and encourage new ones to be built.

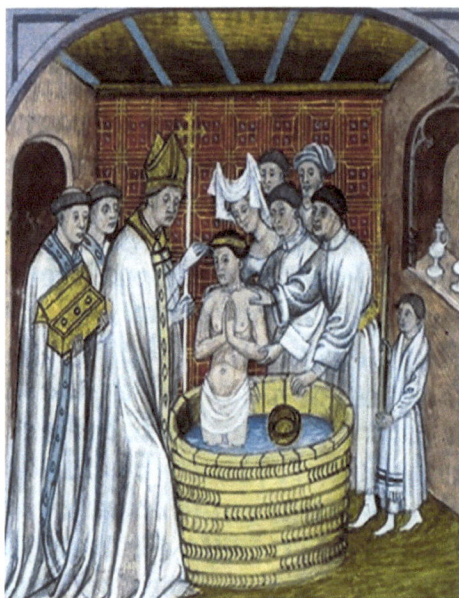

Baptism of Rollo (14th century French manuscript)

The Vikings rapidly integrated into the Frankish majority, adopting their customs and language.

Some Viking laws were introduced such as the Counts monopoly on shipwrecks and banishment/exile (utlagr). The Viking Thing (assembly or council of free speakers) was never introduced and Rollo seems to have kept most of the power of the fledgling state for himself and a few selected companions.

Some Norse words were adapted into the French language such as vagr = Vague/wave and humarr = homard/lobster. Viking place names in Normandy are in abundance. Most towns and villages ending with tot = symbolise a farm, Yvetot, Ectot, Caltot and so on. The towns of Honfleur and Harfleur are both of Scandinavian origin, Hon = possibly a persons name and Fleur = inlet/cove.

Quillebeuf sur Seine = Kilbow in old Norse means village of the bay. Settlements ending with ville usually take the first part from a Viking personal name, Bierville = Bjorn s town/ville. There are over 100 place names ending in bec, meaning a stream or a slope.

Table of some Viking place names in Normandy

Viking	English	Town / village
tot	farm	Yvetot, Ectot, Formetot
bec	Stream/slope	Briquebec, Foulbec
dale/dal	valley	Oudalle, La dalle
hogue	hill	St Vaast de Hogue, Les Hogue
thuit	cleared area	Bracquethuit

The Norman expansion

The Vikings married and assimilated into the local Frankish population and became Normans. In 923 A.D civil war broke out within the Frankish Empire. King Charles III was deposed in a revolt by some of his nobles led by Robert of Neustria. The Franks fought each other culminating in the battle of Soissons 923 A.D where Robert I was killed by Charles III in single combat. Charles actually lost the battle and was taken prisoner.

Meanwhile Rollo exploited the divisions within the Empire and expanded the Norman state. His troops overran most of what is now lower Normandy, capturing the Bessin and

Bayeux up to the river Vire. He was also ceded Le Mans in Maine, south of Normandy. Norman aggression did not stop there, in 925 A.D according to Flodoard de Reims;

The Normans broke the Treaty and attacked the districts of Amiens and Beauvais

The campaign did not go all their way, the French Count of Vermandois counter attacked and destroyed the Norman settlement of Eu. In the savage battle for the town the Frankish soldiers managed to breach the town s defences and slaughtered all the male inhabitants. The war raged on and probably sometime in 925 A.D Rollo s son William Longsword took over the reins of power from his father. Towards the end of his life Rollo seems to have gone mad. It is said before he died in 932-33 A.D that he ordered the execution and beheading of 100 Christian prisoners to appease the pagan Gods. Clearly although Rollo had been baptised a Christian he had never forgotten his Viking past.

Tomb of Rollo, Rouen Cathedral, Normandy

William I Longsword

William I Longsword Count of Rouen continued his father s work to expand and enhance the power of the Norman State. William first had to suppress internal revolts from within Normandy. In 925 A.D the citizens of Bayeux revolted against his rule and then a more serious threat came from Riuf, a Norman/Viking noble who believed that William had become to Frankish. Riulf led a Viking revival and marched his army to the very gates of the Norman capital Rouen. With the city on the verge of being besieged William sent his pregnant wife Sporta to the safety of the loyalist town of Fecamp on the coast. After continued negotiations, William launched a surprise attack on the rebel camp, scattering the heathens.

William I "Longsword", Falaise

Riulf s army was destroyed and he was forced to flee for his life.

William consolidated his power by coming to terms with King Ralph who granted him permission to annex the **land of the Bretons at the edge of the sea** . This was the Contentin peninsular and the Avranchin. The Contentin was inhabited by Irish-Norwegian Vikings who fought hard against the Count s troops to retain their freedom. The Bretons were forced out of the Avranchin and William resettled the land with a group of Danish warriors under the leadership of Aigrold.

King Ralph died in 936 A.D and Hugh the Great installed Louis (the exiled son of the former King Charles III) on the Frankish throne. Hugh hoped that he could use Louis as a puppet King to further his own ends. Within two years, Louis rebelled against Hugh s guardianship and the Empire was plunged into civil war again.

In 939 A.D William Longsword intervened and invaded the disputed territory of Ponthieu which lay between Normandy and Flanders. The Count of Flanders retaliated and captured the capital of

Arms of Normandy

Ponthieu, Montreuil. The pro-Norman Count of Ponthieu Herluin fled to Normandy and with William s help raised a Norman army. Herluin crossed the frontier and recaptured Montrreuil, slaughtering the Flemish garrison. The tit for tat war continued and William was excommunicated by the Pope for his continued raids on Flanders/France.

Reconciliation came about in 940 A.D when William traveled to Amiens and committed himself to King Louis IV. Two years later William was tricked into attending a peace conference with the Count of Flanders to settle the disputed region of Ponthieu and Montreuil. During the meeting William was murdered by the Count s men. The event caused a power struggle for the very survival of Normandy itself.

Duke Richard I   the fearless

King Louis IV never forgot the loyalty of William Longsword and supported his son (Richard I   the fearless) claim to the Duchy. The Viking Aigold, (William s man in Lower Normandy) also allied himself with Richard. The early years of Richard s reign were filled with constant danger.   In 943 A.D Tormod led an internal rebellion against the Duke and linked up with a Viking invasion fleet from York under the command of Sigfred Sigtryggsson.   Together they headed for Rouen, in the battle that followed Richard and King Louis IV s forces utterly annihilated the rebel and Viking army.   Both Tormod and Sigfred were killed in the fighting, reputedly by the King himself.

Norman castle of Fecamp, Normandy

Richard was the first of the Counts of Rouen to use the title Duke. Relations with the Bretons improved when Conan I Duke/Count of Brittany signed a treaty with Richard. On reaching adulthood with the help of the Norman nobles the Duke managed to distance himself from the politics of the Carolingian Empire and concentrated on strengthening the Duchy of Normandy.

Richard further united ties with the Norman nobility by marrying Gunnora, a reputedly beautiful lady of Danish origin. Legend has it that when the Duke was out hunting he heard of the beauty of forester s wife Seinfreda. The Duke sent out his men to capture her and bring her to him but Seinfreda hid and the soldiers took her unmarried sister Gunnora instead. Richard was extremely happy and took Gunnora to be his mistress. They had seven children together including Richard II Duke of Normandy, Robert who became the Archbishop of Rouen upon the marriage of his parents and Emma of Normandy who married King Æthelred the Unready of England. After his death she then married the Viking King Cnut the Great of Denmark and England.

Feudalism increased under Duke Richard, and as a result Normandy became more organised and united. The Norman adoption of Carolingian cavalry tactics enabled them to sever the link to the Scandinavian style of fighting on foot. Slowly the Norman war machine was emerging as a force to be reckoned with during the beginning of the 11th century.

13th Century manuscript showing Duke Richard and his children

Richard II   the good

When Duke Richard I died in 996 A.D he had ruled Normandy for over half a century. The Duchy passed the hands of his son Duke Richard II the good . Richard was still in his minority, so the reins of power were held by his uncles and his mother Gunnora.

Duke Richard II with the abbots of Mont St Michel

During the first year of his reign, the Norman peasantry revolted. All over the Duchy peasants and free farmers banded together in groups and assemblies. Their objective was to achieve greater liberty and freedom from the increasing demands of the Duke and the aristocracy. Duke Richard II and his half uncle Rudolf D Ivry got word of the growing discontent and brutally crushed the rebellion with vicious zeal. The rebels were captured and had their hands and feet cut off to serve as warning to other would-be troublemakers.

During the reign of Richard II the Norman age of expansion started. Norman adventurers and mercenaries such as the sons of Tancred De Hauteville flocked to Southern Italy to seek fame and fortune (see my book, **THE FIRST MAFIA** The Norman Conquest of Southern Italy and Sicily). A certain Roger De Tosny (later known as Roger de l Espagne) fought against the Moors in Spain. On one such occasion in Iberia, he and a troop of 40 men were ambushed by 500 Moors. Roger fought like a wild boar and killed over 100 of the enemy. When he returned to Normandy a hero, he built the Abbey of Saint Pierre at Conches en Ouche (L Eure).

Richard II supported King Svein Forkbeard of Denmark in his Viking invasion of Anglo-Saxon England, from whom he received a proportion of the spoils. He may even have sent Norman mercenaries to fight in the battle of Clontarf (Ireland). In 1014 A.D the Duke gave refuge to his nephews (the Anglo-Saxon heirs) Alfred and Edward (later King Edward the Confessor of England).

The De Tosny Norman castle of Conches en Ouche, L'Eure

In 1026 A.D Duke Richard died and was buried in the Abbey of Fecamp alongside his father.

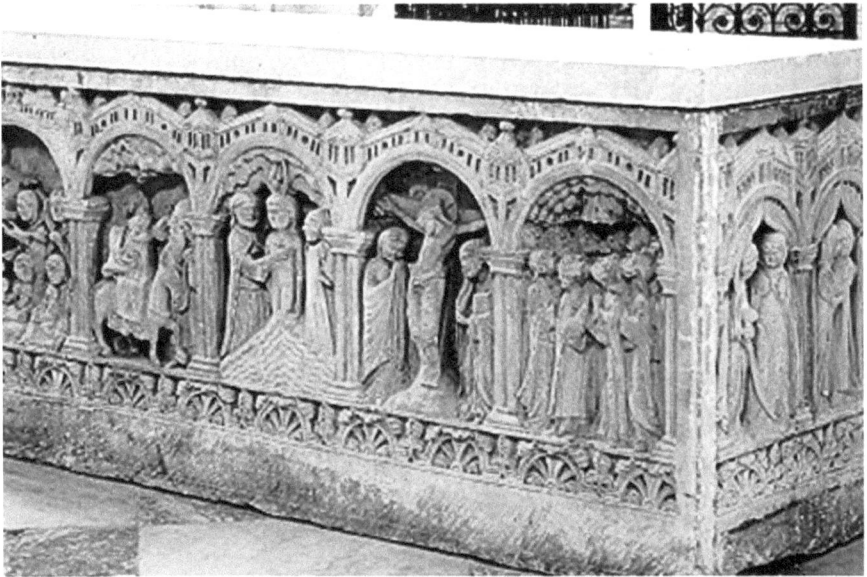

Tomb of the Dukes of Normandy, Richard I, Richard II, Fécamp

Richard III and Robert the Magnificent

Richard III was already an experienced military commander before he was proclaimed Duke. His military skills were put to the test when his brother Robert, who was unhappy with only receiving the County of Hiémois, rebelled against his rule. Richard harried the rebels and laid siege to the great castle of Falaise in lower Normandy. With the odds stacked against him Robert capitulated and made peace with his brother. Richard III returned to the Norman capital Rouen but suddenly became ill and died. Robert who had the most to gain from his brother s death was suspected of poisoning him. Whatever the truth maybe Robert was proclaimed Robert I Duke of Normandy. The New Duke faced various revolts and uprisings from the ever increasing powerful Norman aristocracy, including his Uncle Robert the Archbishop of Rouen, Hugh the Bishop of Bayeux and the Count of

Belleme. But Robert quickly quelled the disturbances and restored order to the Duchy.

Alain III of Brittany took advantage of the internal strife in Normandy and invaded the Avranchin. In a lighting campaign against the Bretons, Robert forced Alain III to submit, acknowledge him as his overlord and concede Brittany as a vassal state of the Dukes of Normandy. The Duke also helped and gave military assistance to his overlord, the King of France, who bestowed upon him the important region of the Vexin between the river Epte and Oise. At the zenith of his power Robert decided to go on pilgrimage to the Holy land. Before departing he made the Norman nobility accept his illegitimate son, William the bastard is his rightful heir. On the return journey from Jerusalem in 1035 A.D Robert died in Nicaea (Turkey). Later a mission was sent by his son William, to bring his body back to Normandy. When the envoys learned that William had died they decided to intern Robert s body in Norman Auplia (Southern Italy).

Falaise castle, Calvados lower Normandy

The Iron Duke

William II the bastard before the Conqueror

Legend has it that Robert the Magnificent laid eyes on a beautiful young lady from the castle of Falaise. Her name was Herleva/Arlette (the daughter of a tanner or embalmer). Apparently she was dying leather garments, and when Robert saw her his lust was uncontrollable. She was brought to the castle where they became lovers.

The legend of Herleva (Robert Wace Roman de Rou)

I dreamt that a tree was coming out of my body and rising up into the sky above; the whole for Normandy was covered by the shadow cast from its branches

Herleva did indeed have something growing in her body and in 1027/1028 A.D she gave birth to a baby boy. The boy was named William and in time his shadow just like in his mother s dream did come true and cover all of Normandy and later England as well.

The fountain of Arlette, below Falaise castle, according to legend this is the exact spot where Robert encountered Arlette.

Duke William II became the Conqueror, the most famous of all the Normans. His Conquest of Anglo-Saxon England earned him a place in history and 1066 A.D still is the most famous date in the island s history. Before William became the Conqueror he was known to his contemporaries as William the bastard . As the illegitimate son of Robert the magnificent , William was catapulted into the limelight when his father died in 1035 A.D.

Robert the Archbishop of Rouen (William s great uncle) upheld the wishes of Duke Robert and proclaimed young William, who was only seven years old, Duke William II of Normandy. William was sent to Paris to perform the act of fealty and homage where he received the consent as the

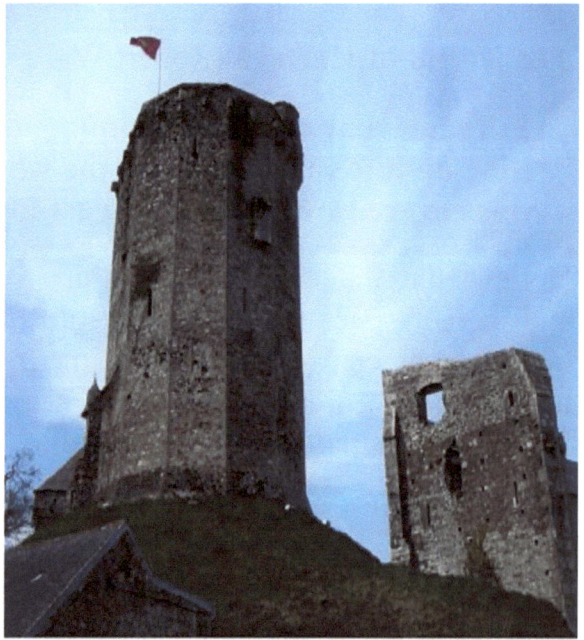

The Norman castle of Bricquebe, Contentin, Normandy

rightful Duke from his overlord King Henry I of France. In March 1037 A.D his great uncle Robert died and the Duchy descended into chaos.

William of Jumieges wrote:

Conspiracies and plots were hatched and the Duchy was ablaze with fire

From the very start of his reign, William s life was in mortal danger. Some of the Norman nobles and even some of William s relatives refused to accept his rule and sought to have him murdered. On one such occasion, Osbern de Crespon (William s guardian and the Seneschal of Normandy) had his throat cut in front of the boy s eyes. In 1042 A.D William was coming of age, he was knighted at the siege of Falaise, where he forced Turstein, the Viscount of Hiémois, to submit and surrender.

In 1046 A.D the conspiracy against the young Duke deepened when Guy de Bourgogne (a grandson of Duke Richard II) and various Norman nobles assembled in Bayeux and swore to destroy William.

Duke William II from an early manuscript

William was resting in the castle of Valognes (Contentin, Western Normandy) when he was awoken by Goles, the court jester who told him he had overheard a plot to kill him. William crept out of the castle and fled on horseback. He continued riding hell-for-leather cross the entire region to reach the safety of Falaise. Under the cover of darkness he passed through the treacherous marshes of the Contentin and crossed the river Vire near the modern day town of Isigny-sur-mer. In the morning William sought refuge with Hubert de Ryes, who gave the young Duke a fresh horse and provisions. Hubert advised William to avoid Bayeux and travel to Falaise via the old Roman road through the Orne valley.

The Norman countryside was swarming with rebel soldiers eager to capture or kill the Duke, but William avoided capture and reached his hometown of Falaise.

The Battle of Val es Dunes 1047

In 1047 A.D William was determined to crush the Western rebels once and for all. With the help of the faithful Norman barons and King Henry of France, the Duke pushed into lower Normandy and prepared to give battle to Guy De Bourgogne, Grimont de Plessis and the remaining rebels. Just outside the great medieval city of Caen the two armies confronted each other.

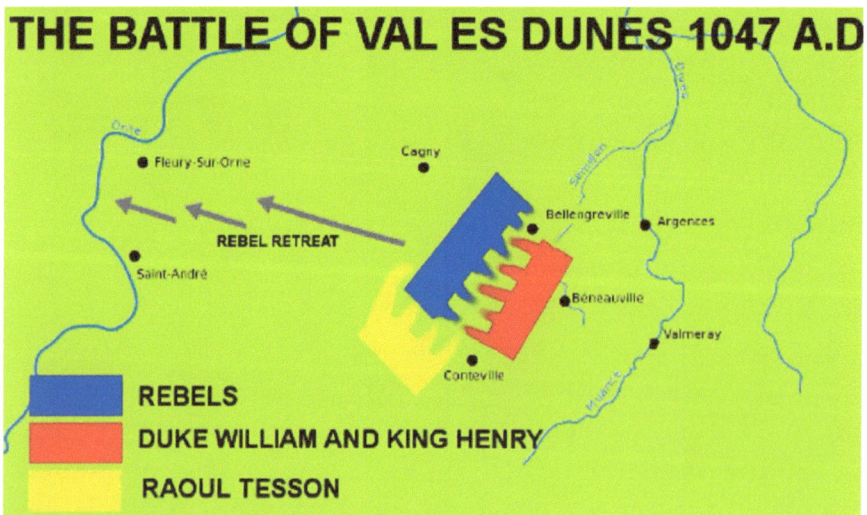

THE BATTLE OF VAL ES DUNES 1047 A.D

REBEL RETREAT

Fleury-Sur-Orne
Cagny
Bellengreville
Argences
Saint-André
Béneauville
Valmeray
Conteville

REBELS
DUKE WILLIAM AND KING HENRY
RAOUL TESSON

Robert Wace, Roman de Rou :

You should have seen the divisions and their leaders stretched out across the vast plains: there was not one Lord nor man of influence present who did not have either a war banner or flag near him. You could have

seen the battlefield tremble, horses were charging into the attack, spears were raised, lances brandished. There was an almighty noise when the two armies clashed, the very ground beneath them was disturbed and shook

Although outnumbered by the rebels, William and King Henry decided to attack. As the loyalist forces advanced a third army came into view. Raoul Tesson de Thury Harcourt had not joined either the rebels or the Duke s forces. Both sides sent urgent envoys to try and convince Raoul and his retinue to commit to their side.

Although Raoul had been one of the rebels who had sworn to destroy William at the secret meeting in Bayeux, in the end he decided that he could not make war against his rightful overlord, Duke William and the King of France. He

Monument to the Battle of Val es Dunes

met the Duke and struck William in the face with his glove. Raoul said: **my oath is complete, I had sworn to smite you and by this act I have. Henceforth I will do you no further harm, for I am your liege man .** Raoul returned to his men and waited on the side lines between the two armies.

The battle commenced with the fully armoured mounted knights riding at full gallop against one another. The chivalry of Normandy now clashed together in the fierce mounted hand to hand combat. The King s division crashed into the rebels from the Contentin. Lances were broken into the bodies of the horses and their riders, and then swords were drawn and plunged into the mail coats of the Norman and French knights.

A rebel Norman knight charged straight through the Royal household and struck King Henry on his hauberk (helmet). The King was beaten off his horse and fell to the ground, unharmed but a little shaken. He immediately remounted and continued to fight in the fray. The better organisation of William and the loyalist forces were holding their own against the overwhelming rebel numbers. William fought like a lion, hacking the limbs off his enemies and killing all in his path.

Norman knight, Temple Pyx

Then two incidents turned the battle in favour of the Duke. One of the rebel s leaders, Haimo/Hamon de Creully, nicknamed Le Dentu was killed in the fighting; his death caused panic amongst his men, who were starting to look for an exit route from the bloody field. Then Raoul Tesson decided the time was right and attacked the rebels in their

rear. Raoul and his men charged in, shouting the war cry
 TUR AIE forging a path deep into the enemy ranks. The
remaining rebels broke formation and fled for their lives.
Many died whilst trying to ford the Orne River, weighed
down by their heavy armour; they drowned in the bloody
water. William relentlessly pursued the rebels, killing and
capturing many men. The victory was complete for the
Duke, who had fought the first major battle of his career.

The rebel leadership had been smashed, but Guy de
Bourgogne escaped and took refuge in the formidable
castle of Brionne in the
valley of the Risle
(Central Normandy).

Many of the surviving,
rebels were pardoned,
but Grimont de Plessis
who had been captured
after the battle trying to
flee to his castle in the
Bessin, was sent to
Rouen and later died in
imprisonment.   A
gruesome   tale
circulated that William,
who hated Grimont had

Brionne keep, not the same castle of Guy de Bourgogne

him torn apart, piece by piece using a wooden knife. He
was skinned, and his skin was made into a saddle cover.

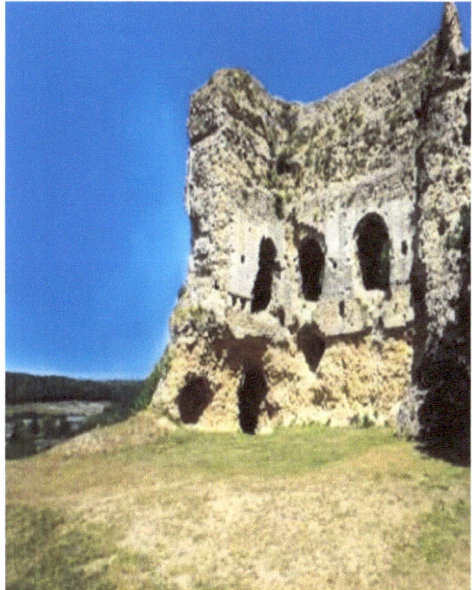

William set about restoring order to the Duchy. Firstly he
besieged Guy s castle of Brionne. The siege lasted for
three years until Guy requested terms of surrender. In the
end he was pardoned and left Normandy to return to
Burgundy.

The Duke also enlisted the help of the church, who agreed to impose the Truce of God . The agreement stated that private wars were forbidden between Wednesday evening and Monday morning. They were entirely prohibited during the holy periods of Advent, Easter, Lent and Pentecost. Only the Duke and the King of France were exempted from the treaty, but anyone else who violated the truce would be excommunicated.

Statue of Matilda, Paris

In 1049 A.D William negotiated with Baldwin of Flanders for the hand of his daughter Matilda, in marriage. When Pope Leo IX heard about this proposal he forbid the marriage on the grounds that William and Matilda were too closely related (both were distant cousins and descendants of Rollo, the Viking founder of Normandy). Pope Leo IX was the same Pope who was defeated and captured after the Battle of Civitate by the Norman Conquerors of Southern Italy (See my book, **THE FIRST MAFIA**). The real reason may have been political, for both the French King and the Holy Roman Emperor Henry III were concerned about the creation of a Norman-Flemish power block in Northern France. William took no notice of the interdiction and went ahead with the marriage. Matilda was escorted to the great frontier town of Eu, where William was waiting for her. In the church of Notre Dame et Saint Laurent d Eu the happy couple was married.

To the south of Normandy, Geoffrey Martel, the Count of Anjou, had been busy extending his domains. He had encroached on the disputed region of Maine, which in the past had acknowledged the Dukes of Normandy as their overlords. When Count Hugh IV of Maine died, Geoffrey seized his chance and took over the entire region, including the strategic castles of Domfront and Alencon on the Norman border.

King Henry of France was growing concerned about the increasing power of both Normandy and Anjou decided to play one side off against the other. He requested William attack the Count lands, hoping both sides would be weakened by the conflict.

Ruins of the castle of Domfront on Normandy's southern border

William launched a major military assault on the castle of Domfront, but was unable to take it by force. On hearing the news from Domfront, the citizens of Alencon, confident of withstanding the Norman attack, hung animal skins from the battlements, in reference to William s ancestry as the illegitimate son of Duke Robert and a tanner's daughter. When the town fell to the Normans, William ordered the leading citizens of the town to be brought before him. For mocking him, he had their hands and feet cut off in front of the rest of the town. When the garrison of Domfront got wind of the story they immediately surrendered under a promise of mercy. William s victory enabled him to annex the Plassais region into the Duchy of Normandy.

William of Poitiers commented that William said in the words of Julius Caesar:

I came, I saw, I conquered

Further insurrections, Arques 1053

No sooner than having returned from his victorious campaign in Southern Normandy, William was faced with yet another insurrection. Since leaving the Norman host during the siege of Domfront, William de Talou (the Duke s uncle) had been busy stirring up trouble for his nephew. From the formidable castle of Arques in Eastern Normandy, he openly defied the Duke. William immediately invaded the county and nearly took the castle by surprise. Arques was too strong to be directly assaulted, so William besieged the castle and blockaded the surrounding area using the loyalist lords of Longueville to supervise the siege. King Henry of France decided to support the rebels covertly, and sent Enguerrand II (son of the Count of Ponthieu) to relieve the siege. William expected such a plan and had stationed a mobile force of mounted knights in the vicinity. As Enguerrand II approached St Aubin, his force was attacked by a small detachment of Norman knights who conducted a feinted flight. Thinking the knights were retreating, Enguerrand II charged after them, not knowing that he was being drawn into an ambush. From the wooded undergrowth around him appeared the main body of William s mobile force. It was carnage as the French soldiers tried in vain to flee the bloody scene. The relief force was completely annihilated including Enguerrand II, who was killed in the melee. The Normans allegedly used the same successful tactic 13 years later at the Battle of Hastings.

With no hope of relief from the outside world, the garrison surrendered in the winter of 1053 A.D. William s rebellious uncles were banished from Normandy never to return again. The King of France, who was left embarrassed by the whole debacle, decided that he would have to lead the army directly against Duke William in the next campaigning season. He formed an alliance with his old enemy, Geoffrey Count of Anjou and planned an invasion set for the spring of 1054 A.D.

The remains of the formidable castle of Arques, Eastern Normandy

The Battle of Mortemer 1054

King Henry I of France and Geoffrey Count of Anjou invaded the Duchy (Evreux region) in early 1054 A.D. While Duke William faced the threat on the south side of the river Seine, the defence of upper Normandy was entrusted to Robert, Count of Eu, William de Warenne, (later 1st Earl of Surrey) Hugh de Gournay, Roger de Mortemer, Hugh de Montfort and Gauthier Giffard. The French incursion was commanded by Count Odo (The King s brother) and Count Rainald of Montdidier.

The invasion force entered the Eastern borders of upper Normandy sacking and pillaging the district in the custom of the time. They captured and encamped within the small town of Mortemer en Bray on their way towards Rouen, to link up with King Henry who had been ravaging the Evreux region. Count Odo was over confident and neglected to secure the area, unaware of the presence of the Norman defence force.

Just before dawn, while the French were still sleeping, the Normans with the local knowledge of Roger de Mortemer, encircled the town, cutting off any escape routes. They then set fire to the thatched houses

Carving of Norman knights, Eardisley church

and buildings. Within minutes the dark sky was ablaze with fire and smoke bellowing out the town s dwellings. The French were in total disarray, and the panic stricken soldiers tried to gather their booty and flee the town. Unfortunately for them, the Norman knights and militia attacked them at this crucial moment, charging out of the darkness into the burning rubble of the town. The battle for Mortemer became a slaughter; in the burning streets the Normans wreaked a bloody revenge on the invaders. By the end of the day the carnage and rout of the French army was complete.

Although Count Odo (King Henry s brother) had managed to escape, many valuable French prisoners were captured including Rainald Count of Montdidier. The battle of Mortemer had inflicted a crushing defeat on the French.

Duke William is said to have thanked God for the victory and sent Ralph de Toeni / Tosny to give the good news to the French King and the Count of Anjou.

The Norman chronicler Orderic Vital reported that Ralph crept up to the French camp and shouted

Mortimer arms, St Laurence church, Ludlow

"FRENCHMEN! FRENCHMEN! ARISE, ARISE! PREPARE FOR FLIGHT, YE SLEEP TOO LONG! AWAY, AND BURY YOUR FRIENDS WHO HAVE BEEN SLAIN AT MORTEMER!"

Overleaf; The Battle of Mortemer 1054 A.D

On hearing the woeful news from Mortemer, King Henry called off the invasion and fled a hastily retreat back across the Norman border.

One of the heroes of the battle was Roger de Mortemer. In the rout that followed he captured Rainald de Montdidier, who was actually his father in law and also his feudal lord for lands within the French kingdom. Roger released the Count, but without the consent of the Duke. William was outraged at the release of an important prisoner and ransom.

Orderic Vital commented that Duke William said:

I banished Roger from Normandy for this offence, but became reconciled with him soon afterwards.

Mortemer was pardoned, and his successors became one of the most powerful Marcher Lord families of the English-Welsh border after the Norman Conquest (see my book **INTO THE DRAGON S LAIR**).

The final showdown, The Battle of Varaville 1057

The Battle of Mortemer practically put an end to the internal divisions within the Duchy. William had only to contend with the outside threat from the King and the Count of Anjou. In 1055A.D William decided to take the offensive against his enemies. He invaded the County of Mayenne situated on Normandy s Southern border. The Duke constructed a new castle at Ambrieres which he intended to be used as a forward base for the

Royal arms of France

conquest of the County. The local lord, Geoffrey de Mayenne, appealed to his overlord Geoffrey Count of Anjou for assistance. The Count headed north and a standoff between the Normans and Angevins ensued. Geoffrey tried in vain to besiege the castle of Ambrieres, but was thwarted by the presence of the Duke s army. He retreated back to Anjou and conspired with King Henry, who was determined to destroy his Vassal William, once and for all.

Monument to the Battle of Varaville 1057

In the summer of 1057 A.D the Royal host of King Henry and the Angevins crossed the border and invaded Normandy. They ravaged the countryside, destroying the corps and burning all the settlements in their wake. Even the city of Caen was sacked. William was gathering his forces in Falaise waiting for the right moment to attack. When his spies brought word to him that the invaders were planning to cross the marshes of the Pays d Auge, the Duke seized his chance and marched out with the army. As the invaders crossed the Dives estuary, laden down with their spoils from the campaign near

Varaville, disaster struck. Duke William waited until half the French had crossed the bridge then gave the signal to attack. The Normans ferociously pounced upon the French rearguard. Caught completely by surprise, the French soldiers tried to force their way over the wooden causeway. Under pressure from the sheer weight and numbers, the bridge collapsed into the rising waters of the estuary. King Henry watched the disaster unfold; he could do nothing but look on in despair, as his army was annihilated. The entire rearguard was killed, captured or drowned. Even the Norman peasants armed with clubs and crude farm weapons joined the battle.

William de Poitiers described the battle;

Caught by complete surprise on this side of the estuary, under the watchful eyes of the King, almost all fell under the strokes of the sword, apart from those who were terrified, and preferred to throw themselves into the waters .

For King Henry it was nothing less than a total disaster. He left Normandy with his tail firmly tucked between his legs, never to return to the Duchy ever again.

Robert Wace commented;

The King went back to France, filled with anger and despair. He no longer bared arms and never again set foot in Normandy.

William s position in Normandy was now stronger than it had ever been. Within two years after the battle of Varaville both King Henry and the Count of Anjou were dead. They were succeeded by infant heirs and William was almost given a free hand to strengthen and enhance the power of the Duchy of Normandy.

The Conquest of Maine 1062

The historic region of Maine lies between Normandy and Anjou with Le Mans as its capital. In 1051 A.D Geoffrey Count of Anjou had banished Count Hebert II who took refuge in Normandy. Herbert II allied himself with William and promised that if he died without issue, his title as Count of Maine would pass to the Duke. William also arranged the marriage between his son Robert and Herbert s younger sister.

The remodelled medieval castle of Sillé-le-Guillaume, Mayenne

In the spring of March 1062 Herbert II died childless in Normandy. William at once gathered his troops and invaded Maine to uphold his claim. The Duke was opposed by his old enemy Geoffrey de Mayenne. The fighting was difficult, but slowly the Normans gained the upper hand.

In 1063 A.D William broke through the defences of Le Mans and entered the capital where he had his son Robert crowned Count. The last sparks of resistance were snuffed out with the capitulation of the great border fortress of Sille le Guilliame and the capture of Geoffrey de Mayenne. A legend states that Geoffrey was held up in the castle of Mayenne with food and provisions. William preferring not to risk a long drawn out siege bribed two children, who entered the castle and set fire to it, forcing Geoffrey to abandon the fortress and surrender.

In 1064 A.D William invaded Brittany and forced Conan II to recognise him as his overlord. In one of the strange coincidences of history, Harold Godwinson actually fought alongside the Duke during this campaign. William had beaten all of his enemies and secured the Duchy against any potential threats. Now he embarked on the greatest gamble of his life, the Conquest of a Kingdom far greater and more prosperous than his own, England (see my book **DOMESDAY 1066** the Norman Conquest and destruction of Anglo-Saxon England)

Normandy after the Conquest of England

In the spring of 1067 A.D William returned to Normandy. No longer was he regarded as William the bastard but as William the Conqueror. Against all the odds the Duke had triumphed and was now the King of England. William began a tour of the Duchy visiting the abbeys of Fecamp, St Pierre sur Dives and Jumieges where he held court. Trouble was brewing in England and by the end of the year William set out to restore order in his new Kingdom.

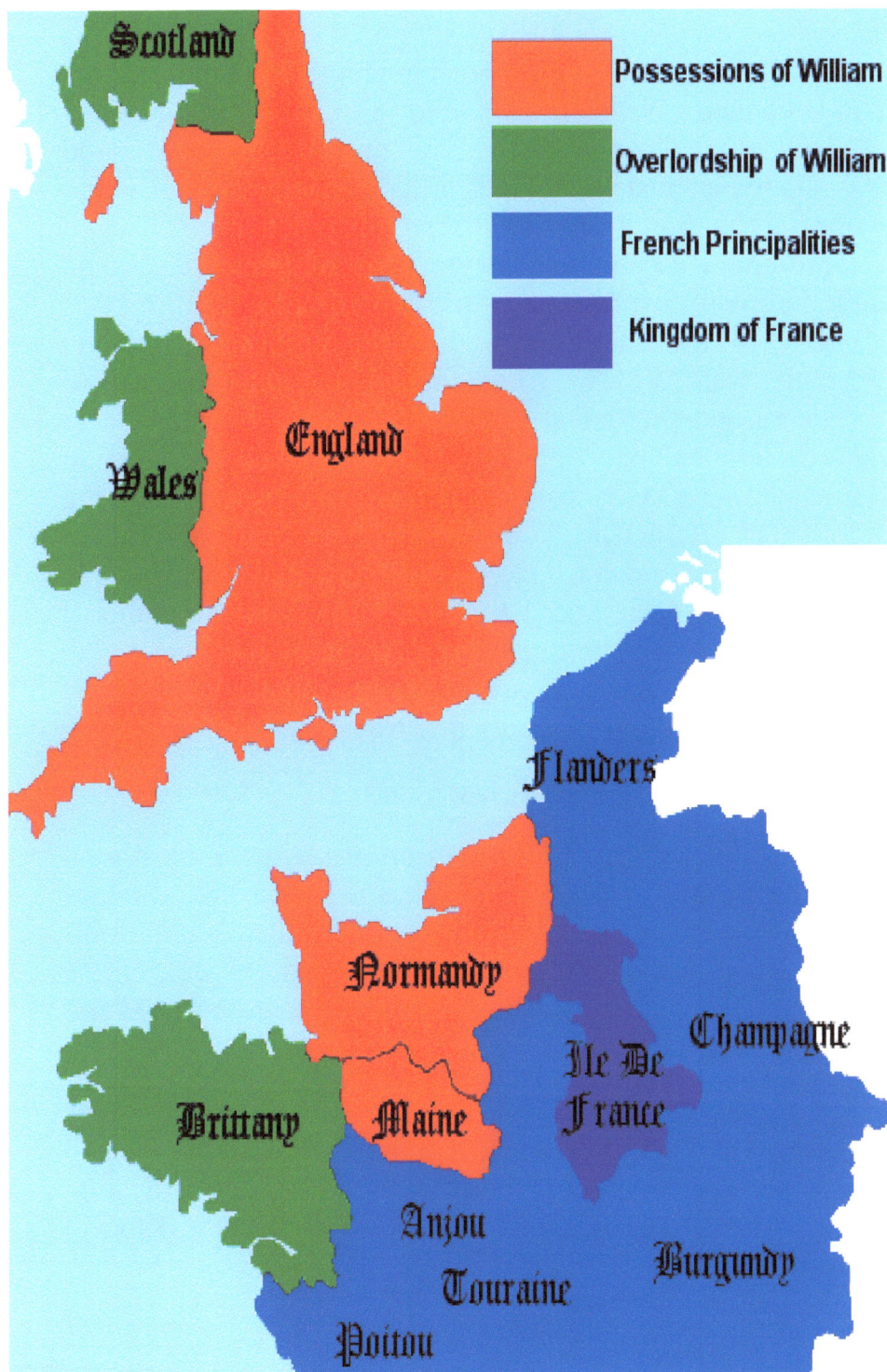

Scotland

Possessions of William

Overlordship of William

French Principalities

Kingdom of France

England

Wales

Flanders

Normandy

Champagne

Ile De France

Brittany

Maine

Anjou

Burgundy

Touraine

Poitou

In 1070 Count Baldwin VI of Flanders (William s brother in-law) died. William supported the claim of his nephew Arnulf to the County, and sent his most trusted loyal friend William Fitz Osbern to look after his interests. Another one of the boy s uncles, Robert, disputed his nephew s claim and with the help of the King of France destroyed the Norman-Flemish forces at the battle of Cassel in 1071 A.D. In the encounter both William Fitz Osbern and Arnulf were killed. Encouraged by the absence of William and the defeat of the Norman forces in Flanders Maine erupted into open revolt and expelled the Norman garrison from Le Mans. William worried by events on the continent returned to Normandy with an army of Norman and English soldiers. He swiftly surprised the rebels in Maine and recaptured Le Mans. In a shrewd political move he defused the threat from Anjou by recognising the Count of Anjou as overlord of Maine, thus leaving Robert his son to control the County free from any interference.

The last years

The last years of William s life were spent mostly in Normandy trying to assert his authority over the advances of his nobles and the King of France. William suffered his first defeat at the hands of the French King at Dol, on the Norman-Breton border. He was forced to lift the siege and retreat back to Normandy. Undeterred William fought on and inflicted a defeat against the Angevins in 1077 AD.

His Son Robert, nicknamed Curthose (probably given to him because he wore short trousers known as Courte heuse) rebelled against his father and joined the King of France.

William is said to have told his son:

It was with Norman valour that enabled me the conquer England, and Normandy is mine by hereditary descent and I will never relinquish it up while I live .

Robert raided Normandy from the castle of Gerberoi on the Norman - Picardie border until his father arrived on the scene and besieged the castle. Legend states that both father and son fought each other beneath the walls of the castle. Robert wounded his father killing his horse from underneath him. William was only saved when an English knight called Tokig of Wallingford, gave the King his horse. William s family troubles continued: his half brother Odo, the Bishop of Bayeux and Earl of Kent was arrested in 1082 A.D for raising an army against the wishes of the King. When Odo pleaded that as a Bishop he could not be arrested, William replied that he was not being arrested as Bishop of Bayeux, but as the Earl of Kent.

The last campaign 1087

In 1087 A.D the aged King set out on his final military campaign. The French garrison of Mantes had crossed the border and raided the Norman Vexin, William was determined to punish the offenders and reclaim the whole of the Vexin which had actually been ceded to his father back in the early part of the 11th century. William crossed the river Epte and harried the land, destroying the crops and vines as he made his way towards Mantes. When the Duke arrived in Mantes the French garrison fled in terror, burning down the town to try and halt the Norman advance. As the Duke ventured through the burning rubble his horse became spooked and threw him against his saddle. William seems to have suffered some internal bleeding and was carried back to the Norman capital Rouen in a litter. Unable to sleep because of the noise of the city William was taken to the priory of St Gevais just outside the city. On the 9th of September 1087 A.D William Duke of Normandy, who had ruled the Duchy for 52 years and had been King of England since 1066 died. William s legacy continued through his sons Robert, William, Henry and his granddaughter Matilda the Empress .

Conclusion

Within 150 years of establishing themselves, The Dukes of Normandy had created one to the most feared and organised Principalities in Medieval Europe. As the 12th century approached, the Viking age was coming to an end. The hour of the Normans had arrived; they would spearhead the invasions and Conquests of Anglo-Saxon England, the Celtic Kingdoms of Wales, Ireland, and Scotland and become Christianities, iron fist in the re-conquest of the Holy-land. However their first expansion took them to the foot of Southern Italy and Sicily. The exploits of the sons of Tancred de Hauteville would become engrained in Norman Myth and legend. The penniless Mafia like mercenaries defied the odds and created the Norman Kingdom in the sun.

Next in the series;

THE FIRST MAFIA
The Norman Conquest of
Southern Italy and Sicily

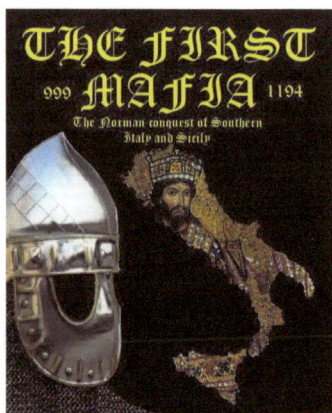

www.ingramcontent.com/pod-product-compliance
Lightning Source LLC
LaVergne TN
LVHW010022070426
835508LV00001B/3